How I was grafted in

Your personal journal recording your
Christian legacy... Past, Present and Future

Anna Kozyra

WestBow
PRESS
A DIVISION OF THOMAS NELSON

WestBow Press books may be ordered through booksellers or by contacting:

WestBow Press
A Division of Thomas Nelson
1663 Liberty Drive
Bloomington, IN 47403
www.westbowpress.com
1-(866) 928-1240

Printed in the United States of America

ISBN: 978-1-4497-2965-3 (e)
ISBN: 978-1-4497-2966-0 (sc)

Library of Congress Control Number: 2011918908

WestBow Press rev. date: 10/26/2011

To Jesus Christ, for EVERYTHING.

To my husband, for always inspiring me and for his constant love and support in everything I do.

To my dad and his God-given talent of art.

To my mom, for my foundation, which allowed me to build upon the Rock.

And to all who were instrumental in getting me to where I am today—

I love you.

This journal is a living testimony of your
Christian legacy—past, present, and future.

It's your personal interactive journal that you
create and share how you came to know Jesus
Christ as your personal Lord and Savior.

Use it to document your walk, challenges and victories,
spiritual growths, testimonies and relationships.

You will record who touched your life and who touched
theirs, going back and going forward with your mission of
winning souls for the Lord and interacting with others.

Everyone has a story that needs to be shared.

Record yours today. Share, learn, and grow with
others, and set up your legacy in the Kingdom.

This book will go on and on and on ...

How I came to meet Jesus Christ as my personal Lord and Savior:

_____

_____

_____

_____

_____

_____

_____

_____

_____

_____

_____

_____

_____

Your Tree

Place names onto the tree and write their testimonies on the corresponding pages. Start with you, and go back as far as you can to see how you came to be grafted into the kingdom.

How you were grafted in ...

Your Branches

(the people who came before you and their stories and testimonies)

Your Branches

Your Branches

_____

_____

_____

_____

_____

_____

_____

_____

_____

_____

_____

_____

_____

Your Branches

Your Branches

_____

_____

_____

_____

_____

_____

_____

_____

_____

_____

_____

_____

_____

Your Branches

Notes

My Church

My Home Church _____

My Pastor _____

Phone _____

Ministries

_____

_____

_____

_____

_____

_____

_____

_____

_____

_____

_____

My Baptisms

On this page, write about your own baptism and other baptisms you have attended.

_____

_____

_____

_____

_____

_____

_____

_____

_____

_____

_____

_____

Churches I Have Visited

Church _____

Pastor _____

Title of Sermon _____

Scripture Verse _____

Notes

_____

_____

_____

_____

_____

_____

_____

_____

_____

_____

Church _____

Pastor _____

Title of Sermon _____

Scripture Verse _____

Notes

_____

_____

_____

_____

_____

_____

_____

_____

_____

_____

Church _____

Pastor _____

Title of Sermon _____

Scripture Verse _____

Notes

_____

_____

_____

_____

_____

_____

_____

_____

_____

_____

_____

Church _____

Pastor _____

Title of Sermon _____

Scripture Verse _____

Notes

_____

_____

_____

_____

_____

_____

_____

_____

_____

_____

_____

Church _____

Pastor _____

Title of Sermon _____

Scripture Verse _____

Notes

_____

_____

_____

_____

_____

_____

_____

_____

_____

_____

_____

_____

Church _____

Pastor _____

Title of Sermon _____

Scripture Verse _____

Notes

_____

_____

_____

_____

_____

_____

_____

_____

_____

_____

_____

My Favorite Sermon

My Favorite Scriptures

Growing God's Kingdom

Your Tree

Place names onto the tree and write their testimonies on the corresponding pages.

Start with you, and go forward with how the Lord is using you to help build His kingdom.

From the smallest of all seeds ...

The kingdom of heaven is like a mustard seed ...

Your Branches

(the people coming after you, and their stories and testimonies)

Your Branches

Your Branches

Your Branches

Go ye into all the world ...

Things the Lord has spoken to me

John 10:27: "My sheep hear my voice, and I know them, and they follow me."

Weeds

Things I need to overcome

Romans 12:21: "Be not overcome of evil, but overcome evil with good."

Weed Killers

Things I have overcome and the people or circumstances that have led me to my victory in these areas

Hebrews 12:1: "Wherefore seeing we also are compassed about with so great a cloud of witnesses, let us lay aside every weight, and the sin which doth so easily beset us, and let us run with patience the race that is set before us."

Missions

Romans 10:14–15: "How then shall they call on him in whom they have not believed? And how shall they believe in him of whom they have not heard? And how shall they hear without a preacher? And how shall they preach, except they be sent? As it is written, how beautiful are the feet of them that preach the gospel of peace, and bring glad tidings of good things!"

Missions I have supported

Prayer Requests

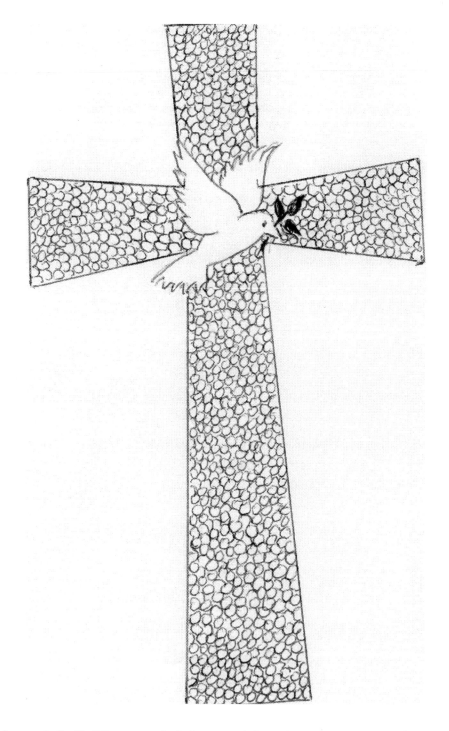

Philippians 4:6–7: "Be careful for nothing, but in everything by prayer and supplication with thanksgiving let your requests be known unto God and the peace of God, which passeth all understanding, shall keep your hearts and minds through Christ Jesus."

Person for prayer   **Prayer request**

_____

_____

_____

_____

_____

_____

_____

_____

_____

_____

_____

_____

_____

Person for prayer

Prayer request

Person for prayer   **Prayer request**

_____

_____

_____

_____

_____

_____

_____

_____

_____

_____

_____

_____

_____

Directory

Name	Address	Phone

Name	Address	Phone

Name	Address	Phone

Bible studies

Date _____

Speaker _____

Sermon Title _____

Scripture Verse _____

Notes

_____

_____

_____

_____

_____

_____

_____

_____

_____

_____

Date _____

Speaker _____

Sermon Title _____

Scripture Verse _____

Notes

_____

_____

_____

_____

_____

_____

_____

_____

_____

_____

Date _____

Speaker _____

Sermon Title _____

Scripture Verse _____

Notes

_____

_____

_____

_____

_____

_____

_____

_____

_____

_____

_____

Date _____

Speaker _____

Sermon Title _____

Scripture Verse _____

Notes

_____

_____

_____

_____

_____

_____

_____

_____

_____

_____

_____

Date _____

Speaker _____

Sermon Title _____

Scripture Verse _____

Notes

_____

_____

_____

_____

_____

_____

_____

_____

_____

_____

_____

_____

Date _____

Speaker _____

Sermon Title _____

Scripture Verse _____

Notes

_____

_____

_____

_____

_____

_____

_____

_____

_____

_____

Date _____

Speaker _____

Sermon Title _____

Scripture Verse _____

Notes

_____

_____

_____

_____

_____

_____

_____

_____

_____

_____

_____

Date _____

Speaker _____

Sermon Title _____

Scripture Verse _____

Notes

_____

_____

_____

_____

_____

_____

_____

_____

_____

_____

_____

Date _____

Speaker _____

Sermon Title _____

Scripture Verse _____

Notes

_____

_____

_____

_____

_____

_____

_____

_____

_____

_____

_____

_____

2 Timothy 4:7–8

"I have fought a good fight, I have finished my course, I have kept the faith: Henceforth there is laid up for me a crown of righteousness, which the Lord, the righteous judge, shall give me at that day: and not to me only, but unto all them also that love his appearing."